Common Biometrics Vocabulary
CBV v1.0

I0450443

Core Terminology

Biometric	Of or having to do with biometrics.
	ISO/IEC 2382-37:2012(E)
	Reviewed and Approved by: BEAWG March 2013

Biometric Encounter	A biometric encounter occurs when a biometric sample(s) is captured from an individual or a latent biometric sample(s) is collected.
	Derived From: DoD BEWL
	Reviewed and Approved by: BEAWG March 2013

Biometric Identity	A biometric identity is established when a biometric sample(s) is used instead of a name to identify a Person of Interest (POI). The biometric identity may consist of the results of one or more biometric encounters for the same individual.
	Derived From: DoD BEWL
	Reviewed and Approved by: BEAWG March 2013

Biometric Sample	A biological specimen or a representation (e.g. digital, analog etc.) of biometric characteristics prior to biometric feature extraction.
	Derived From: ISO/IEC 2382-37:2012(E)
	Reviewed and Approved by: BEAWG March 2013

Biometrically Enabled Watchlist (BEWL)	Any list of person of interests (POI), with individuals identified by biometric sample instead of by name and the desired/recommended disposition instructions for each individual.
	Derived From: DoD BEWL
	Reviewed and Approved by: BEAWG March 2013

Biometrics	A general term used alternatively to describe a characteristic or a process. As a characteristic: The measure of a biological (anatomical and physiological) and/or behavioral biometric characteristic that can be used for automated recognition. As a process: Automated methods of recognizing an individual based on the measure of biological (anatomical and physiological) and/or behavioral biometric characteristics.
	Derived From: IBIA Glossary
	Reviewed and Approved by: BEAWG March 2013

Identity	The set of attribute values (i.e. characteristics) by which an entity (e.g., human, application, device, service or process) is recognizable and is sufficient to distinguish that entity from any other entity.
	DoD Biometrics CONOPS
	Reviewed and Approved by: BEAWG March 2013

Latent Fingerprint	A fingerprint 'image' left on a surface that is dormant or hidden until circumstances are suitable for development or manifestation. (Example: The transferred impression is left by the surface contact with the friction ridges, usually caused by the oily residues produced by the sweat glands in the finger.)
	See Also: Fingerprint Scanning.
	Derived From: IBIA Glossary
	Reviewed and Approved by: BEAWG March 2013

Latent Sample	A biological residue that is dormant, inactive, or non-evident but can be captured, measured and stored.
	Derived From: DoD Biometrics CONOPS
	Reviewed and Approved by: BEAWG March 2013

DoD Biometrics Enterprise Architecture (Integrated) v2.0
Common Biometric Vocabulary (CBV)

A Common Vocabulary is a collection of key terms and definitions used by a specific Community of Interest (COI) to promote common understanding and use.	
Name	The DoD Biometrics Enterprise Architecture (Integrated) v2.0 (BioEA)
Architect	Defense Forensics and Biometrics Agency (DFBA) Architecture Branch
Developed By	DFBA Programs Division
Overview[1]	As per DODAF 2.0, when a specific community has its own local vocabulary which uses terms in different ways from other communities, it is documented in a common vocabulary so that terms can be consistently defined, understood and used across all viewpoints, models and views within the Architectural Description. The vocabulary should include notes on any unique definitions used and provide a mapping to standard definitions, where and when applicable.

Detailed Description

The Common Biometrics Vocabulary (CBV) is a collection of key biometrics terms and definitions commonly used by the DoD Biometrics Enterprise and its Community of Interest (COI). A COI is the inclusive term used to describe a collaborative group of users who must exchange information in pursuit of their shared goals, interests, missions, or business processes and who therefore must have a shared vocabulary for the information they exchange.[2] The CBV will promote a common lexicon for DoD Biometrics stakeholders to reference and use in:

- Development of materials required in the Joint Capabilities Integration Development System (JCIDS) process.
- Updating of Doctrine, Organization, Training, Materiel, Leadership and Education, Personnel and Facilities (DOTMLPF).
- Communication amongst the community as well as with other U.S. Government and International stakeholders.
- Development of integrated architectures across DOTMLPF spectrum that are in conformance with the approved Biometrics Enterprise Architecture (BioEA).

A term will be considered for inclusion in CBV if it meets one or more of the following criteria:

- Term is required for development of other architectures for conformance.
- Term has inadequate coverage in a published standard, commonly accepted dictionary or other DoD recognized authoritative source.
- Term has definition different from one in an existing DoD recognized authoritative source but has unique use of this term agreed upon by the BioEA COI (via the BioEA Working Group COI).

One of the primary goals of the COI is to develop and maintain semantic and structural agreements to ensure that data assets can be understood and used effectively by COI members and unanticipated users.[3] To satisfy this goal, the CBV is arranged in two sections (CORE and SUPPORTIVE) with an appendix.

- **Core Terminology**: These are the terms that address specific understanding of information being exchanged within the Biometrics Enterprise.
- **Supportive Terminology**: These are the terms that support a common understanding of the execution of biometric operations within the Biometrics Enterprise.

The appendix has a section for each of the following:

- **Acronyms:** Cross reference to acronyms used in descriptions within the terminology.
- **References:** Full description of primary source references used to define the term name and definition.
- **Mappings:** List of Core CBV terms mapped to BioEA DIV-2 (Logical Data Model) Entities. This provides a deeper understanding of the information/data relationship between the core CBV terms and the BioEA's DIV-2 entities.

The CBV is not intended to define scientific or technical biometrics terms that describe how the biometric science is conducted; or other DoD terminology that is not biometrics or forensic specific. The BioEA AV-2 contains terms that are specific to the architecture and defines the objects depicted in the architecture. The CBV is meant to complement the terms defined in the AV-2. Together the CBV and AV-2 are comprehensive recordings of the biometrics vocabulary from both business and architecture perspectives.

Each Term in the CBV will contain the following components:

- *Term Name* – Name of term (and Acronym if applicable).
- *Description* – Definition for the term name.
- *Reference* – Primary source used to define the term name and definition.
- *Reviewed and Approved by* – Authoritative Body who last reviewed and approved term content.

All terminology in the CBV reviewed and approved by the BEAWG will be maintained as part of the BioEA with the BEAWG as the governing body, and therefore is the authoritative source of DoD biometrics terminology for the Biometrics COI.

---

[1] Overview quoted, paraphrased and/or otherwise derived from the Department of Defense Architecture Framework (DODAF) Version 2.0 Volume II
[2] Community of Interest (COI) as described in the DoD Net-Centric Data Strategy, 9 May 2003
[3] As described in the Guidance for Implementing Net-Centric Data Sharing (DoD 8320.02-G), 12 April 2006

Supportive Terminology

A

American National Standards Institute (ANSI)	A private, non-profit organization that administers and coordinates the U.S. voluntary standardization and conformity assessment system. The mission of ANSI is to enhance both the global competitiveness of U.S. business and the U.S. quality of life by promoting and facilitating voluntary consensus standards and conformity assessment systems, and safeguarding their integrity.
	IBIA Glossary
	Reviewed and Approved by: BEAWG March 2013
Analyze	The capability and/or process to convert data to actionable information and recommendations as applicable to increase situational awareness and better understand possible courses of action.
	For example, to deliberately consider available information on an individual and reach logical conclusions. These conclusions can include his intent, affiliation(s), activities, location and behavioral patterns.
	Derived From: DoD Biometrics CONOPS
	Reviewed and Approved by: BEAWG March 2013
ANSI/NIST-ITL	The American National Standards Institute (ANSI) National Institiute of Standards and Technology (NIST) - Information Technology Laboratory (ITL) is a standard that defines the content, format, and units of measurement for the exchange of biometric sample information that may be used in the identification or verification process of a subject.
	Derived From: ANSI/NIST-ITL 1-2011
	Reviewed and Approved by: BEAWG March 2013
Arch	A friction ridge pattern in which the friction ridges enter from one side, make a rise in the center, and exit on the opposite side. The pattern will contain no true delta point.
	See Also: Fingerprint.
	Derived From: IBIA Glossary
	Reviewed and Approved by: BEAWG March 2013
Armed Forces DNA Identification Laboratory (AFDIL)	A division of the Office of the Armed Forces Medical Examiner under the Armed Forces Institute of Pathology. Provides scientific consultation, research and education services in the field of forensic DNA analysis to the Department of Defense and other agencies, as well as worldwide, and DNA reference specimen collection, accession, and storage of United States military and other authorized personnel.

AFDIL website

Reviewed and Approved by: BEAWG March 2013

Associated Information	Non-biometric information about a person. For example, a person's name, personal habits, age, current and past addresses, current and past employers, telephone number, email address, place of birth, family names, nationality, education level, group affiliations, and history, including such characteristics as nationality, educational achievements, employer, security clearances, financial and credit history.

CONOPS for DoD Biometrics Identity Superiority

Reviewed and Approved by: BEAWG March 2013

Authoritative Source	The primary DoD-approved repository of biometric information on a biometric subject. The authoritative source provides a strategic capability for access to standardized, comprehensive, and current biometric files within the DoD and for the sharing of biometric files with Joint, Interagency, and designated Multinational partners. The DoD may designate authoritative sources for various populations consistent with applicable law, policy and directives.

Derived From: DoD Biometrics CONOPS

Reviewed and Approved by: BEAWG March 2013

Automated Biometric Identification System (ABIS)	Generic term for any automated biometric identification system. See Also: Automated Fingerprint Identification System (AFIS), Integrated Automated Fingerprint Identification System (IAFIS), DoD Automated Biometric Identification System (DoD ABIS), Automated Biometric Identification System (IDENT).

Derived From: IBIA Glossary

Reviewed and Approved by: BEAWG March 2013

Automated Fingerprint Identification System (AFIS)	A highly specialized biometric system that compared a submitted fingerprint record (usually of multiple fingers) to a database of records, to determine the identity of an individual. AFIS was predominantly used for law enforcement, but was also being used for civil applications (e.g. background checks for soccer coaches, etc). AFIS has been succeeded by ABIS.

Derived From: IBIA Glossary

Reviewed and Approved by: BEAWG March 2013

Automated Identification Management System (AIMS)	A system that acts as a central web-based informational portal between U.S. Central Command (USCENTCOM), National Ground Intelligence Center (NGIC), and the Defense Forensics and Biometrics Agency (DFBA) that is designed to fuse intelligence analysis and value added comments from field users of matched biometric and biographic data.

USCENTCOM BISA CONOPS

Common Biometrics Vocabulary
CBV v1.0

Reviewed and Approved by: BEAWG March 2013

B

Behavioral Biometric Characteristic	A biometric characteristic that is learned and acquired over time rather than one based primarily on biology. All biometric characteristics depend somewhat upon both behavioral and biological characteristic. Examples of biometric modalities for which behavioral characteristics may dominate include signature recognition and keystroke dynamics.
	IBIA Glossary
	Reviewed and Approved by: BEAWG March 2013

Bifurcation	The point in a fingerprint where a friction ridge divides or splits to form two ridges.
	See Also: Fingerprint.
	IBIA Glossary
	Reviewed and Approved by: BEAWG March 2013

Binning	The process of parsing or classifying data in order to accelerate and/or improve biometric matching.
	Derived From: IBIA Glossary
	Reviewed and Approved by: BEAWG March 2013

Biographic Data	Data that describes physical and non-physical attributes of a biometric subject from whom biometric sample data has been collected. For example, full name, age, height, weight, address, employers, telephone number, email address, birthplace, nationality, education level, group affiliations, also data such as employer, security clearances financial and credit history.
	Derived From: USCENTCOM BISA CONOPS
	Reviewed and Approved by: BEAWG March 2013

Biological Biometric Characteristic	A biometric characteristic based primarily on an anatomical or physiological characteristic, rather than a learned behavior. All biometric characteristics depend somewhat upon both behavioral and biological characteristics. Examples of biometric modalities for which biological characteristics may dominate include fingerprint and hand geometry.
	IBIA Glossary
	Reviewed and Approved by: BEAWG March 2013

Biometric Analysis Packet (BAP)	A Biometrics enabled Intelligence (BEI) product that provides identities of personnel who are biometrically enrolled or watch listed for a specified location. The BAP also provides a brief background summary of the personalities associated with the individual.
	Derived From: Handbook No. 11-25

Reviewed and Approved by: BEAWG March 2013

Biometric Automated Toolset Army (BAT-A)	A multimodal biometric system that collects, stores, and shares fingerprints, iris images, and facial photography. It is used to enroll, identify, and track persons of interest, build digital dossiers on individuals that can include attached digital images, documents, and a wide variety of reports such as: biographic, contextual, relationship, and interrogation reports. BAT-A has an internal biometric signature search/match capability and can be configured into either a mobile or handheld configuration.
	DoD Biometrics CONOPS
	Reviewed and Approved by: BEAWG March 2013
Biometric Capture Device	A device that collects a signal from a biometric characteristic and converts it to a captured biometric sample.
	ISO/IEC 2382-37:2012(E)
	Reviewed and Approved by: BEAWG March 2013
Biometric Capture Process	Process of collecting or attempting to collect signals from a biometric characteristic and converting them to a captured biometric sample.
	ISO/IEC SC37-n-3068
	Reviewed and Approved by: BEAWG March 2013
Biometric Characteristic	A biological and/or behavioral characteristic of a biometric subject that can be detected and from which distinguishing, repeatable biometric features can be extracted for the purpose of automated recognition of biometric subjects.
	Derived From: ISO/IEC SC37-n-3068
	Reviewed and Approved by: BEAWG March 2013
Biometric Characteristics Examiner	An individual with authority to assess biometric characteristics and who does so for the purpose of resolving a biometric claim.
	ISO/IEC 2382-37:2012(E)
	Reviewed and Approved by: BEAWG March 2013
Biometric Data Block	A block of data with a defined format that contains one or more biometric samples or biometric templates.
	ISO/IEC SC37-n-3068
	Reviewed and Approved by: BEAWG March 2013
Biometric Data Capture Attempt	The presentation of a single set of biometric samples to a biometric system for identification or verification. Some biometric systems permit more than one attempt to identify or verify an individual.

Derived From: IBIA Glossary

Reviewed and Approved by: BEAWG March 2013

Biometric Database	A collection of one or more computer files. For biometric systems, these files could consist of biometric sensor readings, templates, match results, related biometric subject information, etc.

Derived From: IBIA Glossary

Reviewed and Approved by: BEAWG March 2013

Biometric Feature	Numbers or labels extracted from biometric samples and used for comparison.

ISO/IEC 2382-37:2012(E)

Reviewed and Approved by: BEAWG March 2013

Biometric Feature Extraction Process	A process applied to a biometric sample with the intent of isolating and outputting repeatable and distinctive numbers or labels which can be compared to those extracted from other biometric samples.

ISO/IEC 2382-37:2012(E)

Reviewed and Approved by: BEAWG March 2013

Biometric Identification System for Access (BISA)	A biometric and contextual data collection and credential card production system.

Derived From: CONOPS for DoD Biometrics Identity Superiority

Reviewed and Approved by: BEAWG March 2013

Biometric Identity Intelligence Resource (BI2R)	Automated database that stores biometric and associated intelligence data from DoD collection devices. Analysts use the BI2R toolset to conduct analysis and develop intelligence reports supporting DoD and national missions. The system is designed to provide the DoD, Intelligence Community (IC), and coalition communities with authoritative, high pedigree, biometrically base-lined identities, and advanced tools and technologies necessary to analyze, collaborate, produce, disseminate, and share biometric identity intelligence.

See Also: AIMS, BIR

Derived From: TC 2-22.82 Biometrics-Enabled Intelligence

Reviewed and Approved by: BEAWG March 2013

Biometric Intelligence Analysis Report (BIAR) BIARs are first phase analytical products that provide current intelligence assessments on individuals who have been biometrically identified at least once and who may pose a threat to US interests. BIARs provide a summary and background on a person's biometric encounters, all-source intelligence analysis, assessments of the subject's threat and intelligence value, summary of actions taken by the analytical element and recommended actions for operators.

Biometrics Identity Management JCD Glossary

Reviewed and Approved by: BEAWG March 2013

Biometric Model	Stored function (dependent on the biometric data subject) generated from a biometric feature(s).

ISO/IEC SC37-n-3068

Reviewed and Approved by: BEAWG March 2013

Biometric Property	The descriptive attributes of the biometric subject estimated or derived from the biometric sample by automated means. Example: Fingerprints can be classified by the biometric properties of ridge-flow, i.e. arch whorl and loop types. In the case of facial recognition, this could be estimates of age or gender.

ISO/IEC 2382-37:2012(E)

Reviewed and Approved by: BEAWG March 2013

Biometric Reference	One or more known stored biometric samples, biometric templates or biometric models attributed to a biometric subject and used for comparison. Example: Face image on a passport; fingerprint minutia(e) template on a National ID card; Gaussian Mixture Model for speaker recognition, in a database.

Derived From: ISO/IEC 2382-37:2012(E)

Reviewed and Approved by: BEAWG March 2013

Biometric Sample Collector	An individual performing the biometric sample collection.

Biometrics Identity Management JCD Glossary

Reviewed and Approved by: BEAWG March 2013

Biometric Standards	Biometric Standards are agreed upon formats established by the DoD internal as well as external authoritative agencies (e.g. ANSI/NIST), that provide rules, guidelines, and characteristics for biometric activities and their results. Interoperability is facilitated by the standards as they establish the size, configuration, or protocol of biometric products, processes, and systems. Biometric Standards specify: 1. Formats for the interchange of biometric data. 2. Common files format that provide platform independence and separation of transfer syntax from content definition. 3. Application program interfaces and application profiles. 4. Performance metric definitions and calculations. 5. Approaches to test performance. 6. Requirements for reporting the results of performance tests.

Reviewed and Approved by: BEAWG March 2013

Biometric Subject	An individual from which biometric samples were collected.
	DFBA
	Reviewed and Approved by: BEAWG March 2013
Biometric System	Multiple individual components (such as sensor, matching algorithm, and result display) that combine to make a fully operational system. A biometric system is an automated system capable of: 1. Capturing a biometric sample from a biometric subject. 2. Extracting and processing the biometric data from that sample. 3. Storing the extracted information in a database. 4. Comparing the biometric data with data contained in one or more references. 5. Deciding how well they match and indicating whether or not an identification or verification of identity has been achieved. A biometric system may be a component of a larger system.
	Derived From: IBIA Glossary
	Reviewed and Approved by: BEAWG March 2013
Biometric Template	Set of stored biometric features comparable directly to biometric features of a recognition biometric sample. NOTE 1: A biometric reference consisting of an image, or other captured biometric sample, in its original, enhanced or compressed form, is not a biometric template. NOTE 2: The biometric features are not considered to be a biometric template unless they are stored for reference.
	ISO/IEC SC37-n-3068
	Reviewed and Approved by: BEAWG March 2013
Biometrically Enabled Physical Access	The process of granting access to installations and facilities through the use of biometrics.
	Derived From: DoD Biometrics CONOPS
	Reviewed and Approved by: BEAWG March 2013
Biometrics Enterprise	The Biometrics Enterprise is an entity comprised of the Department's joint, Service, and Agency organizations working together to integrate biometrics into the identity transactions needed to support military operations and departmental business functions.
	DoD Biometrics Enterprise Strategic Plan
	Reviewed and Approved by: BEAWG March 2013
Biometrics Program	All systems, interfaces, acquisition programs, processes, and activities that are utilized to establish identities of people through the use of biometrics

modalities.

DoDD 8521.01E

Reviewed and Approved by: BEAWG March 2013

C

Closed-set Identification	A biometric task where an unidentified biometric subject is known to be in the database and the system attempts to determine his/her identity. Performance is measured by the frequency with which the biometric subject appears in the system's top rank (or top 5, 10, etc.).
	See Also: Open-set Identification
	Derived From: IBIA Glossary
	Reviewed and Approved by: BEAWG March 2013

Collect	The capability and/or process to capture biometric sample(s) and related contextual data from a scene and/or a biometric subject, with or without his or her knowledge.
	See Also: DoD Biometrics Process.
	Derived From: CONOPS for DoD Biometrics Identity Superiority
	Reviewed and Approved by: BEAWG March 2013

Combined DNA Index System (CODIS)	Both a program and software tool used by the FBI, distributed over three hierarchical levels – National, State and Local Index Systems – that enables state and local law enforcement crime laboratories to exchange and compare DNA profiles electronically.
	FBI NDIS
	Reviewed and Approved by: BEAWG March 2013

Common Biometric Exchange Formats Framework specification (CBEFF)	This standard specifies a common set of data elements necessary to support multiple biometric technologies and to promote interoperability of biometric-based application programs and systems by allowing for biometric data exchange. These common data elements can be placed in a single file, record, or data object used to exchange biometric information between different system components and applications. This standard specifies the biometric data elements.
	CBEFF ANSI INCITS 398-2008
	Reviewed and Approved by: BEAWG March 2013

Comparison	Process of comparing a biometric biometric probe feature(s) with a previously stored reference or references in order to make an identification or verification decision.
	Derived From: IBIA Glossary
	Reviewed and Approved by: BEAWG March 2013

Contextual Data	Elements of biographic data and situational information (who, what, when, where, how, why, etc.) associated with a collection event and permanently

recorded as an integral component of the biometric file.

Derived From: DoD Biometrics CONOPS

Reviewed and Approved by: BEAWG March 2013

| Core Point | The 'center(s)' of a fingerprint. In a whorl pattern, the core point is found in the middle of the spiral/circles. In a loop pattern, the core point is found in the top region of the innermost loop. More technically, a core point is defined as the topmost point on the innermost upwardly curving friction ridgeline. A fingerprint may have multiple cores or no cores. |

See Also: Fingerprint.

IBIA Glossary

Reviewed and Approved by: BEAWG March 2013

| Covert Collection | Collection of biometrics without the knowledge of an individual. An instance in which biometric samples are being collected at a place and/or time that is not known to the subjects. An example of a covert environment might involve an airport checkpoint where facial images of passengers are captured and compared to a watchlist without their knowledge. |

See Also: Overt Collection

Derived From: JointPub

Reviewed and Approved by: BEAWG March 2013

D

Data Source	A specific device, part of the computer or data asset (e.g. data set, file, website, database etc.) where data is stored electronically and from which data can be obtained.
	Derived From: DoD Biometrics CONOPS
	Reviewed and Approved by: BEAWG March 2013

Decide/Act	Take action based on a biometric file's match results and analysis of associated information.
	See Also: DoD Biometrics Process.
	DoD Biometrics CONOPS
	Reviewed and Approved by: BEAWG March 2013

Defense Biometrics Identification System (DBIDS)	A DoD owned and operated system developed by Defense Manpower Data Center (DMDC) as a force protection program to manage installation access control for military installations.
	Derived From: DBIS
	Reviewed and Approved by: BEAWG March 2013

Delta Point	The part of a fingerprint pattern that looks similar to the Greek letter delta. Technically, it is the point on a friction ridge at or nearest to the point of divergence of two type lines, and located at or directly in front of the point of divergence.
	See Also: Fingerprint.
	IBIA Glossary
	Reviewed and Approved by: BEAWG March 2013

Detainee Reporting System (DRS)	A System designed to support the processing of prisoner of war (POWs) and detainees.
	Derived From: DRS
	Reviewed and Approved by: BEAWG March 2013

Detection Error Trade-off Curve (DET)	A graphical plot of measured error rates. DET curves typically plot matching error rates (false non-match rate vs. false match rate) or decision error rates (false rejection rate vs. false acceptance rate).
	Derived From: IBIA Glossary

Reviewed and Approved by: BEAWG March 2013

Difference Score	A value returned by a biometric algorithm that indicates the degree of difference between a biometric sample and a reference.
	IBIA Glossary
	Reviewed and Approved by: BEAWG March 2013

DNA Source	The individual or material from which a DNA sample can be collected or extracted.
	DNA
	Reviewed and Approved by: BEAWG March 2013

DoD Automated Biometric Identification System (DoD ABIS)	DoD ABIS is the central, authoritative, multi-modal biometric data repository. The system operates and enhances associated search and retrieval services and interfaces with existing DoD and interagency biometrics systems. The repository interfaces with collection systems, intelligence systems and other deployed biometric repositories across the federal government.
	New ABIS Improves Capability to Identify Terrorists Press Release
	Reviewed and Approved by: BEAWG March 2013

DoD Electronic Biometric Transmission Specification (DoD EBTS)	The DoD EBTS is a transmission specification to be used between DoD systems that capture biometric data and repositories of biometric data. The DoD EBTS does not attempt to specify all data used in all biometric enabled applications. It does allow for the definition of application specific data elements and transactions.
	DoD EBTS v2.0
	Reviewed and Approved by: BEAWG March 2013

Duplicate Enrollment Check	The comparison of a recognition biometric sample/biometric feature/biometric model to some or all of the biometric references in the enrollment database to determine if any similar biometric reference exists.
	See Also: Enrollment.
	ISO/IEC SC37-n-3068
	Reviewed and Approved by: BEAWG March 2013

E

Electronic Fingerprint Transmission Specification (EFTS)	The original document that specified requirements to which agencies must adhere to communicate electronically with the Federal Bureau of Investigation (FBI) Integrated Automated Fingerprint Identification System (IAFIS). The specification facilitated timely fingerprint information sharing and eliminated the delays associated with fingerprint cards.

This specification has been replaced by the Electronic Biometric Transmission Specification (EBTS).

See Also: FBI Electronic Biometric Transmission Specification |
	Derived From: IBIA Glossary
	Reviewed and Approved by: BEAWG March 2013
Enroll	Create and store, for a biometric subject, an enrollment data record that includes biometric reference(s) and typically, non-biometric data.
	Derived From: ISO/IEC SC37-n-3068
	Reviewed and Approved by: BEAWG March 2013
Enrollment	The process of collecting contextual data and a biometric sample from a biometric subject, converting the sample into a biometric reference, and storing the data in the biometric system's database for later comparison.

See Also: Duplicate Enrollment Check, Full Enrollment, Re-enrollment, Tactical Enrollment. |
| | Derived From: IBIA Glossary |
| | Reviewed and Approved by: BEAWG March 2013 |
| Entire Joint Image (EJI) | An exemplar image containing all four full-finger views for a single finger: one rolled; left, center, and right plain .

See Also: Full Finger View |
| | Derived From: ANSI/NIST-ITL 1-2011 |
| | Reviewed and Approved by: BEAWG March 2013 |
| Equal Error Rate (EER) | A statistic used to show biometric performance, typically when operating in the verification task. The EER is the location on a ROC or DET curve where the false acceptance rate and false rejection rate (or one minus the verification rate {1-VR}) are equal. In general, the lower the equal error rate value, the higher the accuracy of the biometric system. Note, however, that most operational systems are not set to operate at the "equal error rate" so the measure's true usefulness is limited to comparing biometric system performance. The EER is sometimes referred to as the "Crossover Error Rate."

See Also: Detention Error Trade-off Curve (DTE), False Rejection Rate (FRR), |

Detection and Identification Rate, False Non-Match Rate (FNMR), Identification Rate, and Verification Rate

Derived From: Report of the Defense Science Board Task Force on Defense Biometrics

Reviewed and Approved by: BEAWG March 2013

Exemplar	The friction ridge prints of an individual, associated with a known or claimed identity, and deliberately recorded electronically, photographically, by ink, or by another medium.

See Also: Fingerprint.

Derived From: ANSI/NIST-ITL 1-2011

Reviewed and Approved by: BEAWG March 2013

F

Face Recognition	A biometric modality that uses an image of the visible physical structure of a biometric subject's face for recognition purposes.
	See Also: Modality.
	Derived From: IBIA Glossary
	Reviewed and Approved by: BEAWG March 2013

Failure to Enroll (FTE)	Failure of a biometric system to form a proper enrollment reference for an end user. Common failures include end users who are not properly trained to provide their biometrics, the sensor not capturing information correctly, or captured sensor data of insufficient quality to develop a template.
	Derived From: IBIA Glossary
	Reviewed and Approved by: BEAWG March 2013

False Acceptance	When a biometric system incorrectly identifies a biometric subject or incorrectly authenticates a biometric subject against a claimed identity.
	Derived From: NIAP
	Reviewed and Approved by: BEAWG March 2013

False Acceptance Rate (FAR)	A statistic used to measure biometric performance when operating in the verification task. The percentage of times a system produces a false acceptance, which occurs when a biometric subject is incorrectly matched to another biometric subject's existing biometric sample. Example: Frank claims to be John and the system verifies the claim.
	Derived From: IBIA Glossary
	Reviewed and Approved by: BEAWG March 2013

False Match	The comparison decision of 'match' for a biometric probe and a biometric reference that are from different biometric capture subjects NOTE: It is recognized that this definition considers the false match at the subject level only, and not at the biometric characteristic level. Sometimes a comparison may be made between a biometric probe and a biometric reference from different biometric characteristics of a single biometric capture subject. In some of these cases - for example when comparing Galton ridges of different fingers of the same biometric data subject - a comparison decision of 'match' might be considered to be an error, while in other cases - for example when comparing a mispronounced pass-phrase in text-dependent speaker recognition - a comparison decision of 'match' might be considered to be correct.
	ISO/IEC 2382-37:2012(E)
	Reviewed and Approved by: BEAWG March 2013

False Match Rate (FMR)	Proportion of the completed biometric non-match comparison trials that result in a false match.

NOTE 1: The value computed for the false match rate will depend on thresholds, and other parameters of the comparison process, and the protocol defining the biometric non-mated comparison trials.
NOTE 2: Comparisons between:
- identical twins;
- different, but related biometric characteristics from the same individual, such as left and right hand topography will need proper consideration. See ISO/IEC 19795-1.
NOTE 3: 'Completed' refers to the computational processes required to make a comparison decision, i.e. failures to decide are excluded. |
| | ISO/IEC 2382-37:2012(E) |
| | Reviewed and Approved by: BEAWG March 2013 |
| False Non-Match | A comparison decision of 'non-match' for a biometric probe and a biometric reference that are from the same biometric capture subject and of the same biometric characteristic.
NOTE: There may need to be consideration on how much non-conformance to system policy on the part of the biometric capture subject is tolerated before the probe biometric sample and the biometric reference are deemed to be of different biometric characteristics. |
| | ISO/IEC 2382-37:2012(E) |
| | Reviewed and Approved by: BEAWG March 2013 |
| False Non-Match Rate (FNMR) | Proportion of the completed biometric mated comparison trials that result in a false non-match.
NOTE 1: The value computed for the false non-match rate will depend on thresholds, and other parameters of the comparison process, and the protocol defining the biometric mated comparison trials.
NOTE 2: "Completed" refers to the computational processes required to make a comparison decision, i.e. failures to decide are excluded. |
	ISO/IEC 2382-37:2012(E)
	Reviewed and Approved by: BEAWG March 2013
False Rejection	The failure of a biometric system to identify a biometric subject or to verify the legitimate claimed identity of a biometric subject.
	Derived From: NIAP
	Reviewed and Approved by: BEAWG March 2013
False Rejection Rate (FRR)	A statistic used to measure biometric performance when operating in the verification task. The percentage of times the system produces a false rejection. A false rejection occurs when a biometric subject is not matched to his/her own existing biometric template. Example: John claims to be John, but the system incorrectly denies the claim.

Derived From: IBIA Glossary

Reviewed and Approved by: BEAWG March 2013

FBI Electronic Biometric Transmission Specification (FBI EBTS)	The FBI EBTS specifies the file and record content, format, and data codes necessary for the exchange of fingerprint, palmprint, photo, facial, iris and other contextual (biographic and/or situational) information between federal, state, and local users and the FBI/CJIS. It provides a description of all requests and responses associated with electronic fingerprint identification service and other services. As FBI/CJIS moves to NGI, this specification is being re-organized into User Services that include the following: 1. Identification Service 2. Verification Service 3. Information Service 4. Investigation Service 5. Notification Service 6. Data Management Service

Derived From: CJIS EBTS v9.4

Reviewed and Approved by: BEAWG March 2013

FBI Universal Latent Workstation (ULW)	Software program developed by the Federal Bureau of Investigation's (FBI) Criminal Justice information Services (CJIS) Division that, when installed on a commercial off-the-shelf computer, allows the operator to create a native feature set for Automated Fingerprint Identification System (AFIS) vendors by which the Integrated Automated Fingerprint Identification System (IAFIS) can receive and search an ANSI/NIST-formatted record.

AFIS Glossary

Reviewed and Approved by: BEAWG March 2013

Features	Distinctive mathematical characteristic(s) derived from a biometric sample; used to generate a reference.

IBIA Glossary

Reviewed and Approved by: BEAWG March 2013

Fingerprint	An impression of the friction ridges of all or any part of the finger.

See Also: Arch, Bifurcation, Core Point, Delta Point, Exemplar, Friction Ridge, Loop, Minutia(e), Minutia(e) Point, Platen, Ridge Ending, Slap Fingerprint, Ten Print Match, Valley, Whorl.

SWGFAST Document #19, 24 Nov 2012

Reviewed and Approved by: BEAWG March 2013

Fingerprint Recognition	A biometric and forensic modality that uses the physical structure of a biometric subject's fingerprint for recognition purposes. Important features used in most fingerprint recognition systems are minutia(e) points that include bifurcations and ridge endings.

See Also: Modality.

Derived From: IBIA Glossary

Reviewed and Approved by: BEAWG March 2013

Fingerprint Scanning	Acquisition and recognition of a biometric subject's fingerprint characteristics for identification purposes. This process allows the recognition of a biometric subject through quantifiable physiological characteristics that detail the unique identity of an individual.

See Also: Fingerprint Vendor Technology Evaluation, Flat Fingerprint, Latent Fingerprint, Plain Fingerprint, Platen, Rolled Fingerprint, Slap Fingerprint, Ten Print Match.

Derived From: Fingerprint Sensor Product Guidelines

Reviewed and Approved by: BEAWG March 2013

Flat Fingerprint	Fingerprint taken in which the finger is pressed down on a flat surface but not rolled. Also known as Plain Fingerprint.

See Also: Fingerprint Scanning.

Derived From: Latent Fingerprint Matching

Reviewed and Approved by: BEAWG March 2013

Friction Ridge	The ridges present on the skin of the fingers and toes, and on the palms and soles of the feet, which make contact with an incident surface under normal touch. On the fingers, the distinctive patterns formed by the friction ridges that make up the fingerprints.

See Also: Fingerprint.

IBIA Glossary

Reviewed and Approved by: BEAWG March 2013

Friction Ridge Examiner	A person who analyzes, compares, evaluates, and verifies friction ridge impressions.

SWGFAST Document #19, 24 Nov 2012

Reviewed and Approved by: BEAWG March 2013

Full Enrollment	Enrollment of biometric data on a subject that includes 14 fingerprint images (4 slaps, 10 rolls), 5 face photos, 2 irises, and required text fields. The sample must be EBTS compliant. Typically used for detainees, local hire screenings, and other applications.

See Also: Enrollment.

Reviewed and Approved by: BEAWG March 2013

Full Finger View

A full finger view is a rolled or plain image of a full-length finger showing all segments (distal, medial, and proximal segments) of the finger.

See Also: Entire Joint Image

ANSI/NIST-ITL 1-2011

Reviewed and Approved by: BEAWG March 2013

G

Gait	A biometric subject's manner of walking. This behavioral characteristic is in the research and development stage of automation.
	See Also: Modality.
	Derived From: IBIA Glossary
	Reviewed and Approved by: BEAWG March 2013

Gallery	The biometric system's database, or set of known biometric subjects, for a specific implementation or evaluation experiment.
	Derived From: IBIA Glossary
	Reviewed and Approved by: BEAWG March 2013

H

Hamming Distance (HD)	The number of non-corresponding digits in a string of binary digits; used to measure dissimilarity. Hamming distances are used in many Daugman iris recognition algorithms.
	IBIA Glossary
	Reviewed and Approved by: BEAWG March 2013
Hand Geometry Recognition	A biometric modality that uses the physical structure of a biometric subject's hand for recognition purposes.
	See Also: Modality.
	Derived From: IBIA Glossary
	Reviewed and Approved by: BEAWG March 2013

I

Identification Rate	A statistic used to measure biometric performance when operating in the identifcation task. The rate at which legitimate biometric subjects are correctly identified.
	Derived From: IBIA Glossary
	Reviewed and Approved by: BEAWG March 2013

Identifier	A unique data string used as a key in the biometric system to name a biometric subject's identity and its associated attributes. An example of an identifier would be a passport number.
	Derived From: NIAP
	Reviewed and Approved by: BEAWG March 2013

Identity Claim	A statement that a biometric subject is or is not the source of a reference in a database. Claims can be positive (I am in the database), negative (I am not in the database), or specific (I am end user 123 in the database).
	Derived From: IBIA Glossary
	Reviewed and Approved by: BEAWG March 2013

Identity Intelligence	Information produced by the discovery, management, and protection of Identity attributes in support of U.S. national and homeland security interests.
	DA G2
	Reviewed and Approved by: BEAWG March 2013

Identity Superiority	The management, protection and dominance of identity information for friendly, neutral or unknown, and adversary personnel through the application of military operations and business functions.
	CONOPS for DoD Biometrics Identity Superiority
	Reviewed and Approved by: BEAWG March 2013

Individual	As used in the Biometrics Enterprise, an individual refers to a single human being.
	Derived From: ISO/IEC SC37-n-3063
	Reviewed and Approved by: BEAWG March 2013

| Integrated Automated Fingerprint Identification System   (IAFIS) | The FBI's original large-scale ten fingerprint (open-set) identification system that was used for criminal history background checks and identification of latent prints discovered at crime scenes. This system provided automated and latent search capabilities, electronic image storage, and electronic exchange of fingerprints and responses. It is currently in the process of being gradually |

succeeded by the Next Generation Identification (NGI) system.

Derived From: IBIA Glossary

Reviewed and Approved by: BEAWG March 2013

Intermediate Biometric Sample Processing	Any manipulation of a biometric sample that does not produce biometric features.
	Example: Intermediate biometric samples may have been enhanced for biometric feature extraction.
	ISO/IEC SC37-n-3068
	Reviewed and Approved by: BEAWG March 2013
International Association for Identification (IAI)	Professional association whose members are engaged in forensic identification, investigation, and scientific examination of physical evidence.
	AFIS Glossary
	Reviewed and Approved by: BEAWG March 2013
International Biometrics & Identification Association (IBIA)	The International Biometrics & Identification Association (IBIA) is a trade association founded in September 1998 in Washington, DC that promotes the effective and appropriate use of technology to determine identity and enhance security, privacy, productivity, and convenience for individuals, organizations, and governments.
	IBIA Glossary
	Reviewed and Approved by: BEAWG March 2013
International Committee for Information Technology Standards (INCITS)	Organization that promotes the effective use of information and communication technology through standardization in a way that balances the interests of all stakeholders and increases the global competitiveness of the member organizations.
	IBIA Glossary
	Reviewed and Approved by: BEAWG March 2013
Iris Code©	A biometric feature format used in the Daugman iris recognition system.
	IBIA Glossary
	Reviewed and Approved by: BEAWG March 2013
Iris Recognition	A biometric modality that uses an image of the physical structure of a biometric subject's iris for recognition purposes.
	See Also: Modality.
	Derived From: IBIA Glossary

Common Biometrics Vocabulary
CBV v1.0

Reviewed and Approved by: BEAWG March 2013

J

Joint Personal Identification (JPI)	Provides a joint solution to portable biometrics collection for the Department of Defense. Provides capability to capture an individual's biometric data and to positively identify and verify the identity of actual or potential adversaries. The capability is intended to support identity dominance across the full spectrum of operations for all Services. The capability will be used in two major variants, a portable (hand-held) version for use in the field and a mobile version for forward garrison use.

Derived From: JPI CDD

Reviewed and Approved by: BEAWG March 2013

K

Keystroke Dynamics	A potential biometric modality that uses the cadence of a biometric subject's typing pattern for recognition.
	See Also: Modality.
	Derived From: IBIA Glossary
	Reviewed and Approved by: BEAWG March 2013

L

Live Capture	Typically refers to a fingerprint capture device that electronically captures fingerprint images using a sensor (rather than scanning ink-based fingerprint images on a card or lifting a latent fingerprint from a surface).
	See Also: Live Scan
	IBIA Glossary
	Reviewed and Approved by: BEAWG March 2013
Live Scan	An electronic method of taking and transmitting fingerprints without using ink, which produces fingerprint impressions of high quality to perform identification processing.
	See Also: Live Capture
	AFIS Glossary
	Reviewed and Approved by: BEAWG March 2013
Liveness Detection	A technique used to ensure that the biometric sample submitted is from a living biometric subject.
	Derived From: IBIA Glossary
	Reviewed and Approved by: BEAWG March 2013
Local Trusted Source	A sub-set of the Authoritative Source and is established to accomplish a specific function within an operational mission or business process. Reasons for establishing a local trusted source might include: insufficient network connectivity to provide immediate access to the authoritative source, an operational need for closed-loop access, permission application.
	Derived From: DoD Biometrics CONOPS
	Reviewed and Approved by: BEAWG March 2013
Local Un-Trusted Source	A local repository of biometric files that that have not been enrolled with an authoritative or local trusted source. In many cases, local un-trusted sources are established for missions of short duration or to satisfy political, policy, or legal restrictions related to the sharing of biometric information.
	DoD Biometrics CONOPS
	Reviewed and Approved by: BEAWG March 2013
Loop	A friction ridge pattern in which the friction ridges enter from either side, curve sharply and pass out near the same side they entered. This pattern will contain one core and one delta.
	See Also: Fingerprint.

Common Biometrics Vocabulary
CBV v1.0

Derived From: IBIA Glossary

Reviewed and Approved by: BEAWG March 2013

M

Manage	The capability and/or process to perform administrative duties related to biometrics, such as tracking transaction status and transaction logging.
	Biometrics Identity Management JCD Body
	Reviewed and Approved by: BEAWG March 2013

Match	The capability and/or process to compare biometric data in order to link previously obtained biometrics and related contextual data to a particular identity for identification or verification of identity.
	Biometrics Identity Management JCD Body
	Reviewed and Approved by: BEAWG March 2013

Match Result	Comparison decision stating that the biometric probe(s) and the biometric reference are from the same source.
	Derived From: ISO/IEC 2382-37:2012(E)
	Reviewed and Approved by: BEAWG March 2013

Minutia Exchange (MINEX)	MINEX is a series of National Institute of Standards and Technology (NIST) coordinated development efforts aimed at improving the performance and interoperability of core implementations of the INCITS 378 and ISO/IEC 19794-2 fingerprint minutia standards. MINEX 04 is designed to evaluate whether various populations and combinations of encoding schemes, probe templates, gallery templates, and fingerprint matchers will produce successful matches. MINEX II is the part of the MINEX program dedicated to the evaluation and development of the capabilities of fingerprint minutia matchers running on ISO/IEC 7816 smart cards.
	NIST/MINEX
	Reviewed and Approved by: BEAWG March 2013

Minutia(e)	Friction ridge characteristics which occur at points where a single friction ridge deviates from an uninterrupted flow. Deviation may take the form of ending, bifurcation, or a more complicated "composite" type.
	See Also: Fingerprint.
	Derived From: AFIS Glossary
	Reviewed and Approved by: BEAWG March 2013

Minutia(e) Point	The point where a friction ridge begins, terminates, or splits into two or more ridges.
	See Also: Fingerprint.
	ANSI/NIST-ITL 1-2007

Reviewed and Approved by: BEAWG March 2013

Modality	A type or class of biometric sample originating from a biometric subject. For example: face recognition, fingerprint recognition, iris recognition, etc.
	See Also: Face Recognition, Fingerprint Recognition, Hand Geometry Recognition, Iris Recognition, Palm Print Recognition, Speaker Recognition, DNA Matching, Gait, Hand Scan, Keystroke Dynamics, Signature Dynamics.
	Derived From: DoD Biometrics CONOPS
	Reviewed and Approved by: BEAWG March 2013
Mugshot	A photograph of an individual's face. Term used interchangeably with facial image. The term facial image usually implies a higher resolution image than a mugshot.
	Derived From: ANSI/NIST-ITL 1-2007
	Reviewed and Approved by: BEAWG March 2013
Multimodal Biometric System	A biometric system in which two or more of the modality components (biometric characteristic, sensor type or feature extraction algorithm) occurs in multiple.
	DoD Biometrics CONOPS
	Reviewed and Approved by: BEAWG March 2013

N

National DNA Index System (NDIS)	One component of the Combined DNA Index System (CODIS) and the national and highest level index containing the DNA records contributed from participating federal, state and local laboratories.
	FBI QA
	Reviewed and Approved by: BEAWG March 2013

National Information Exchange Model (NIEM)	The National Information Exchange Model is a partnership of the U.S. Department of Justice, the Department of Homeland Security (DHS) and the Department of Health and Human Services (HHS) which provides a framework for information exhchange using an Extensible Markup Language (XML) based message exchange format. It is designed to develop, disseminate and support enterprise-wide information exchange standards and processes that can enable jurisdictions to effectively share critical information in emergency situations, as well as support the day-to-day operations of agencies throughout the nation.
	Derived From: ANSI/NIST-ITL 1-2011
	Reviewed and Approved by: BEAWG March 2013

National Institute of Standards and Technology (NIST)	A non-regulatory federal agency within the U.S. Department of Commerce that develops and promotes measurement, standards, and technology to enhance productivity, facilitate trade, and improve the quality of life. NIST's measurement and standards work promotes the well-being of the nation and helps improve, among many others things, the nation's homeland security.
	NIST
	Reviewed and Approved by: BEAWG March 2013

Next Generation Identification (NGI)	Program to advance the FBI's biometric identification services, providing an incremental replacement of current Integrated Automated Fingerprint Identification System (IAFIS) technical capabilities, while introducing new functionality across a multi-year timeframe.
	AFIS Glossary
	Reviewed and Approved by: BEAWG March 2013

Non-match Result	Comparison decision stating that the biometric probe(s) and the biometric reference are not from the same source.
	Derived From: ISO/IEC 2382-37:2012(E)
	Reviewed and Approved by: BEAWG March 2013

O

One-to-Many Comparison	Comparing one set of biometric probe features to many biometric references to identify a biometric subject. Sometimes referred to as 1: n.
	Derived From: IBIA Glossary
	Reviewed and Approved by: BEAWG March 2013

One-to-One Comparison	Comparing one set of biometric probe features to another biometric reference to identify a biometric subject. Sometimes refered to as 1:1.
	Derived From: IBIA Glossary
	Reviewed and Approved by: BEAWG March 2013

Open-set Identification	Biometric task that more closely follows operational biometric system conditions to 1) determine if a biometric subject is in a database and 2) find the record of the biometric subject in the database. This is sometimes referred to as the "watchlist" task to differentiate it from the more commonly referenced closed-set identification.
	See Also: Closed-set Identification
	Derived From: IBIA Glossary
	Reviewed and Approved by: BEAWG March 2013

Overt Collection	Collection of biometrics with the biometeric subject's knowledge. An example of an overt collection is a fingerprint live scan.
	See Also: Covert Collection
	Derived From: JointPub
	Reviewed and Approved by: BEAWG March 2013

P

Palm Print Recognition	A biometric and forensic modality that uses the physical structure of a biometric subject's palm print for recognition purposes.
	See Also: Modality.
	Derived From: IBIA Glossary
	Reviewed and Approved by: BEAWG March 2013

Palmprint	An impression of the friction ridges of all or any part of the palmar surface of the hand.
	SWGFAST Document #19, 24 Nov 2012
	Reviewed and Approved by: BEAWG March 2013

Person Data Exchange Standard (PDES)	A specification of the U.S. government intelligence community that specifies XML tagging of person data, including biometric data.
	PDES
	Reviewed and Approved by: BEAWG March 2013

Person of Interest (POI)	An individual for whom information needs or discovery objectives exist.
	ODNI
	Reviewed and Approved by: BEAWG March 2013

Personal Identification Number (PIN)	A security method used to show 'what you know.' Depending on the system, a PIN could be used to either claim or verify a claimed identity.
	IBIA Glossary
	Reviewed and Approved by: BEAWG March 2013

Personally Identifiable Information (PII)	Information about an individual that identifies, links, relates, or is unique to, or describes him or her, e.g., a social security number; age; military rank; civilian grade; marital status; race; salary; home/office phone numbers; other demographic, biometric, personnel, medical, and financial information, etc. Also included is such information which can be used to distinguish or trace an individual's identity, such as their name, social security number, date and place of birth, mother's maiden name, biometric records, including any other personal information which is linked or linkable to a specified individual.
	DoDD 5400
	Reviewed and Approved by: BEAWG March 2013

Plain Fingerprint	Fingerprint taken in which the finger is pressed down on a flat surface but not rolled. Also known as Flat Fingerprint.

See Also: Fingerprint Scanning.

Derived From: Latent Fingerprint Matching

Reviewed and Approved by: BEAWG March 2013

Plantar	Having to do with the friction ridge skin on the feet (soles and toes).

EFS

Reviewed and Approved by: BEAWG March 2013

Platen	The surface on which the fingers, toes, palms, or soles of the feet are placed during optical image capture. Platens are also used by other types of electronic fingerprint devices (i.e. capacitive, optical, electro-optical, etc.).

See Also: Fingerprint Scanning.

Derived From: iAfB

Reviewed and Approved by: BEAWG March 2013

Probe	The biometric sample that is submitted to the biometric system to compare against one or more references in the gallery.

IBIA Glossary

Reviewed and Approved by: BEAWG March 2013

R

Receiver Operating Characteristics (ROC)

A method of showing measured accuracy performance of a biometric system. A verification ROC compares false acceptance rate vs. verification rate. An open-set identification (watchlist) ROC compares false alarm rates vs. detection and identification rate.

IBIA Glossary

Reviewed and Approved by: BEAWG March 2013

Recognition

A generic term used in the description of biometric systems (e.g. face recognition or iris recognition) relating to their one to many fundamental function. The term 'recognition' does not inherently imply the verification, closed-set identification or open-set identification (watchlist).

Derived From: IBIA Glossary

Reviewed and Approved by: BEAWG March 2013

Re-enrollment

The process of establishing a new biometric reference for a biometric subject already enrolled in the database.
NOTE: Re-enrollment requires new captured biometric sample(s).

See Also: Enrollment.

ISO/IEC 2382-37:2012(E)

Reviewed and Approved by: BEAWG March 2013

Reference

The capability and/or process of querying various repositories of associated information on individuals (Intelligence, Medical, Human Resources, Financial, Security, Education, Law Enforcement, etc) for analysis purposes.

CONOPS for DoD Biometrics Identity Superiority

Reviewed and Approved by: BEAWG March 2013

Ridge Ending

A minutiae point at the ending of a friction ridge.

See Also: Fingerprint.

IBIA Glossary

Reviewed and Approved by: BEAWG March 2013

Ridge Flow

The direction of one or more friction ridges.

SWGFAST Document #19, 24 Nov 2012

Reviewed and Approved by: BEAWG March 2013

Rolled Fingerprint

An image that includes fingerprint data from nail to nail, obtained by "rolling" the finger across a capture surface.

See Also: Fingerprint Scanning.

Derived From: IBIA Glossary

Reviewed and Approved by: BEAWG March 2013

S

Segmentation	The process of parsing the biometric signal of interest from the entire acquired data system. For example, finding individual finger images from a slap impression.
	IBIA Glossary
	Reviewed and Approved by: BEAWG March 2013

Sensor	Hardware found on a biometric device that converts biometric input into a digital or analog signal and conveys this information to the processing device.
	Derived From: IBIA Glossary
	Reviewed and Approved by: BEAWG March 2013

Share	The capability and/or process to transfer (send and/or receive) biometric sample(s), contextual data, match result and/or associated information within the DoD and between DoD and other national, international, and non-governmental organizations (NGOs) as appropriate and in accordance with applicable laws, policies, authorities and agreements.
	Derived From: DoD Biometrics CONOPS
	Reviewed and Approved by: BEAWG March 2013

Similarity Score	A value returned by a biometric algorithm that indicates the degree of similarity or correlation between a biometric sample and a reference.
	IBIA Glossary
	Reviewed and Approved by: BEAWG March 2013

Situational Information	A component of contextual data that describes the who, what, when, where, how, why, etc. associated with an event and/or subject.
	Derived From: DoD Biometrics CONOPS
	Reviewed and Approved by: BEAWG March 2013

Slap Fingerprint	Fingerprints taken by simultaneously pressing the four fingers of one hand onto a capture surface. Slaps are known as four finger simultaneous plain impressions.
	See Also: Fingerprint Scanning.
	Derived From: IBIA Glossary
	Reviewed and Approved by: BEAWG March 2013

Soft Biometrics	Soft biometric traits are characteristics that provide some identifying information about an individual, but lack the distinctiveness and permanence to sufficiently differentiate any two individuals. Examples of soft biometrics

traits include a person's height, weight, gender, eye color,ethnicity, and SMT.

SMT: Soft Biometric for Suspect and Victim Identification

Reviewed and Approved by: BEAWG March 2013

Speaker Recognition	A biometric modality that uses a biometric subject's speech, a feature influenced by both the physical structure of a biometric subject's vocal tract and the behavioral characteristics of the biometric subject, for recognition purposes. Sometimes referred to as 'voice recognition.' 'Speaker Recognition' is not the same as 'Speech recognition' which recognizes the words being said and is not a biometric technology.

See Also: Modality.

Derived From: IBIA Glossary

Reviewed and Approved by: BEAWG March 2013

Speech Recognition	A technology that enables a machine to recognize spoken words. Speech recognition is not a biometric technology.

IBIA Glossary

Reviewed and Approved by: BEAWG March 2013

Store	The capability and/or process of enrolling, maintaining, and updating biometric files to make available standardized, current biometric sample(s) and contextual data on biometric subjects.

Derived From: CONOPS for DoD Biometrics Identity Superiority

Reviewed and Approved by: BEAWG March 2013

T

Tactical Collection Device (TCD)

A portable system used to capture data that represent biometric characteristics of an individual. The system provides the capability to collect, store, match, share, and manage biometric information and enable a decide/act capability.

TCD and BEC

Reviewed and Approved by: BEAWG March 2013

Tactical Enrollment

Enrollment of biometric data on a subject that includes at least 2 fingerprints (indexes), 2 iris prints, and required text fields. The sample must be EBTS compliant. Typically used when subject is not being detained, but a record of the encounter is required at an IED site, raid, humanitarian assistance, etc. It is an identification leading to an enrollment of a subject utilizing biometric data that includes at least 1 fingerprint or 1 iris and capture identification number.

See Also: Enrollment.

Derived From: Biometrics Identity Management JCD

Reviewed and Approved by: BEAWG March 2013

Ten (10) Print Match or Identification

A positive identification of a biometric subject that is obtained by comparing each of his or her 10 fingerprints to those in a system of record. It is usually performed by an automated fingerprint identification system and verified manually by a human fingerprint examiner.

See Also: Fingerprint Scanning.

DFBA

Reviewed and Approved by: BEAWG March 2013

Terrorist Watchlist Person Data Exchange Standard (TWPDES)

An Extensible Markup Language (XML) based data exchange format for terrorist watchlist data that supports the Department of State, Department of Justice, Intelligence Community under the Director of Central Intelligence, and the Department of Homeland Security. It is designed to develop and maintain, to the extent permissible by law, the most thorough, accurate, and current information possible about individuals known or appropriately suspected to be or have been involved in activities constituting, in preparation for, in aid of, or related to terrorism.

Derived From: TWPDES

Reviewed and Approved by: BEAWG March 2013

Tethered Biometric System

Use of biometric sensors between deployed personnel within a robust command and control architecture.

DFBA

Reviewed and Approved by: BEAWG March 2013

Threshold	A setting for biometric systems operating in the verification or open-set identification (watchlist) tasks. The acceptance or rejection of biometric data is dependent on the match score falling above or below the threshold. The threshold is adjustable so that the biometric system can be more or less strict, depending on the requirements of any given biometric application.
	Derived From: IBIA Glossary
	Reviewed and Approved by: BEAWG March 2013
Transaction	A group of records with information and biometric data concerning a particular individual that is transmitted and/or stored as a complete unit.
	ANSI/NIST-ITL 1-2011
	Reviewed and Approved by: BEAWG March 2013
True Acceptance Rate (TAR)	A statistic used to measure biometric performance when operating in the verification task. The percentage of times a system (correctly) accepts a true claim of identity. For Example, Frank claims to be Frank and the system accepts the claim.
	See Also: True Rejection Rate
	Derived From: IBIA Glossary
	Reviewed and Approved by: BEAWG March 2013
True Rejection Rate (TRR)	A statistic used to measure biometric performance when operating in the verification task. The percentage of times a system (correctly) rejects a false claim of identity. For Example, Frank claims to be John and the system rejects the claim.
	See Also: True Acception Rate
	Derived From: IBIA Glossary
	Reviewed and Approved by: BEAWG March 2013
Type I Error	An error that occurs in a statistical test when a true claim is (incorrectly) rejected. For example, John Claims to be John but the system incorrectly denies his claim .
	See Also: False Rejection Rate
	IBIA Glossary
	Reviewed and Approved by: BEAWG March 2013
Type II Error	An error that occurs in a statistical test when a false claim is (incorrectly) not rejected. For example, Frank Claims to be John but the system verifies the claim .

See Also: True Reject Rate

IBIA Glossary

Reviewed and Approved by: BEAWG March 2013

U

U.S. Visitor and Immigrant Status Indicator Technology (US-VISIT)	The office of U.S. Visitor and Immigrant Status Indicator Technology (US-VISIT) is part of the National Protection and Programs Directorate (NPPD) of the Department of Homeland Security (DHS). US-VISIT supports DHS's responsibility to protect the nation by providing biometric identification services that help federal, state, and local government decision makers accurately identify the people they encounter and determine whether those people pose a risk to the United States.

The office of US-VISIT supplies a continuum of security measures that begins overseas, at the Department of State's visa issuing posts, and continues through arrival and departure from the United States of America. Using biometrics, such as digital, inkless fingerscans and digital photographs, the identity of visitors requiring a visa is now matched at each step to ensure that the person crossing the U.S. border is the same person who received the visa. For visa-waiver travelers, the capture of biometrics first occurs at the port of entry to the U.S. By checking the biometrics of a traveler against its databases, US-VISIT verifies whether the traveler has previously been determined inadmissible, is a known security risk (including having outstanding wants and warrants), or has previously overstayed the terms of a visa. These entry and exit procedures address the U.S. critical need for tighter security and ongoing commitment to facilitate travel for the millions of legitimate visitors welcomed each year to conduct business, learn, see family, or tour the country. |
	Derived From: IBIA Glossary
	Reviewed and Approved by: BEAWG March 2013
United States Army Criminal Investigation Laboratory (USACIL)	USACIL provides forensic laboratory services to DoD investigative agencies and other federal law enforcement agencies.
	USACIL
	Reviewed and Approved by: BEAWG March 2013
Untethered Biometric System	Collection, analysis and use of biometric sensors between deployed personnel outside of a robust command and control architecture.
	DFBA
	Reviewed and Approved by: BEAWG March 2013
US-VISIT/IDENT	The United States Visitor and Immigrant Status Indicator Technology (US-VISIT) Automated Biometric Identification System (IDENT) is a Department of Homeland Security (DHS) wide system for the storage and processing of biometric and limited biographic information for DHS national security, law enforcement, immigration, intelligence, and other DHS mission-related functions.
	Derived From: IDENT
	Reviewed and Approved by: BEAWG March 2013

V

Valley	A lowered portion of the epidermis on the palmar or plantar skin, consisting of those areas between ridges.
	See Also: Fingerprint.
	ANSI/NIST-ITL 1-2011
	Reviewed and Approved by: BEAWG March 2013
Verification	The one-to-one process of matching a biometric subject's biometric sample against his stored biometric file. Also known as Authentication.
	Derived From: CONOPS for DoD Biometrics Identity Superiority
	Reviewed and Approved by: BEAWG March 2013
Verification Rate	A statistic used to measure biometric performance when operating in the verification task. The rate at which legitimate biometric subjects are correctly verified.
	Derived From: IBIA Glossary
	Reviewed and Approved by: BEAWG March 2013

W

Wavelet Scalar Quantization Grayscale Fingerprint Image Compression Specification (IAFIS-IC-0010 [V3]) (WSQ)	Provides the definitions, requirements, and guidelines for specifying the FBI's WSQ compression algorithm. The document specifies the class of encoders required, decoder process, and coded representations for compressed image data.
	CJIS EBTS v9.4
	Reviewed and Approved by: BEAWG March 2013
Whorl	A friction ridge pattern in which the ridges are circular or nearly circular. The pattern will contain 2 or more deltas.
	See Also: Fingerprint.
	Derived From: IBIA Glossary
	Reviewed and Approved by: BEAWG March 2013

Common Biometrics Vocabulary
CBV v1.0

Acronyms

ABIS	Automated Biometric Identification System
AFDIL	Armed Forces DNA Identification Laboratory
AFIS	Automated Fingerprint Identification System
AIMS	Automated Identification Management System
ANSI	American National Standards Institute
AOR	Area of Responsibility
ASCII	American Standard Code for Information Interchange
AV-2	All View 2
BAP	Biometric Analysis Packet
BAT-A	Biometric Automated Toolset
BC	Biometric Consortium
BDT	Biometrics Data Team
BEAWG	Biometrics Enterprise Architecture Working Group
BEC	Biometrics Enabling Capability
BEI	Biometric-Enabled Intelligence
BEWL	Biometrically-enabled Watchlist
BFC	Biometric Fusion Center
BG	Biometrics Glossary
BI2R	Biometric Identity Intelligence Resource
BIAR	Biometric Intelligence Analysis Report
BIMA	Biometrics Identity Management Agency
Bio API	Biometric Application Programming Interface
BioEA	Biometrics Enterprise Architecture
BIR	Biometric Information Record
BIR	Biometric Intelligence Resource
BISA	Biometric Identification System for Access
BMO	Biometric Management Office
BSWG	Biometric Standards Working Group
BTF	Biometrics Task Force
CAC	Common Access Card
CBA	Capabilities Based Assessment
CBEFF	Common Biometric Exchange File Format
CBEFF	Common Biometric Exchange Formats Framework
CE	Communications Equipment
CENTCOM	Central Command
CJIS	Criminal Justice Information Services
CLDM	Core Logical Data Model
CMC	Cumulative Match Characteristic
CMR	Cumulative Match Rate
COCOM	Combatant Command
CODIS	Combined DNA Index System

COI	Community of Interest
CONOPS	Concept of Operations
DBEKS	DoD Biometric Expert Knowledgebase System
DBIDS	Defense Biometric Identification System
DET	Detection Error Tradeoff
DHS	Department of Homeland Security
DMDC	Defense Manpower Data Center
DNA	Deoxyribonucleic Acid
DoD	Department of Defense
DoD ABIS	Department of Defense Automated Biometric Identification System
DoD EBTS	Department of Defense Electronic Biometric Transmission Specification
DoDD	Department of Defense Directive
DPI	Dots Per Inch
DRS	Detainee Reporting System
EER	Equal Error Rate
EFTS	Electronic Fingerprint Transmission Specification
EJI	Entire Joint Image
EMIO	Expanded Maritime Interdiction Operation
FAR	False Acceptance Rate
FBI	Federal Bureau of Investigation
FBI EBTS	Federal Bureau of Investigation Electronic Biometric Transmission Specification
FHA	Foreign Humanitarian Assistance
FMR	False Match Rate
FNMR	False Non Match Rate
FOUO	For Official Use Only
FP	Force Protection
FPVTE	Fingerprint Vendor Technology Evaluation
FRR	False Rejection Rate
FRVT	Face Recognition Vendor Test
FTA	Failure To Acquire
FTE	Failure To Enroll
G2 DA	Office of the Deputy Chief of Staff for Intelligence (ODCSINT) Department of the Army
GMM	Gaussian Mixture Model
HD	Hamming Distance
HMM	Hidden Markov Model
iAfB	International Association for Biometrics
IAFIS	Integrated Automated Fingerprint Identification System
IAI	International Association for Identification
IBIA	International Biometrics & Identification Association
IC MWG	Intelligence Community Metadata Working Group
ICSA	International Computer Security Association
IDD	Integrated Data Dictionary
IDENT	Automated Biometric Identification System - Department of Homeland Security

INCITS	International Committee for Information Technology Standards
IREX	Iris Exchange
ISO	International Organization for Standardization
JCD	Joint Capabilities Document
JPEG	Joint Photographic Experts Group
JPI	Joint Personal Identification
JTC1/SC37	Joint Technical Committee 1, Subcommittee 37, Biometrics
LEP	Locally Employed Personnel
MINEX	Minutia Exchange
mtDNA	Mitochondrial DNA
NDIS	National DNA Index System
nDNA	Nuclear DNA
NGI	Next Generation Identification
NGIC	National Ground Intelligence Center
NIEM	National Information Exchange Model
NIST	National Institute of Standards and Technology
NSA	National Security Agency
NSTC	National Science and Technology Council
ODNI	Office of the Director of National Intelligence
ORCON	Dissemination & Extraction of Information Controlled by Originator
PDES	Person Data Exchange Standard
PII	Personally Identifiable Information
PIN	Personal Identification Number
POI	Person of Interest
PPI	Pixels Per Inch
RAPID	Real-time Automated Personnel Identification System
RFS	Ready For Staffing
ROC	Receiver Operating Characteristics
SCI	Sensitive Compartmented Information
SME	Subject Matter Expert
SWGFAST	Scientific Working Group on Friction Ridge Analysis, Study and Technology
TAR	True Accept Rate
TCD	Tactical Collection Device
TRR	True Reject Rate
TWPDES	Terrorist Watchlist Person Data Exchange Standard
ULW	Universal Latent Workstation
US-VISIT	U.S. Visitor and Immigrant Status Indicator Technology
USACIL	United States Army Criminal Investigation Laboratory
WSQ	Wavelet Scalar Quantization
XML	Extensible Markup Language

References

AFDIL website	Armed Forces DNA Identification Laboratory website
AFIS Glossary	Glossary of AFIS Terms; Latent Print AFIS Interoperability Working Group http://www.nist.gov/oles/upload/AFIS_Glossary-Rev-02-05012012.pdf
ANSI/NIST-ITL 1-2007	ANSI/NIST-ITL 1-2007, Data Format for the Interchange of Fingerprint, Facial, & Scar mark & Tattoo Information http://www.nist.gov/itl/iad/ig/ansi_standard.cfm
ANSI/NIST-ITL 1-2011	ANSI/NIST-ITL 1-2011, NIST Special Publication 500-290 Data Format for the Interchange of Fingerprint, Facial & Other Biometric Information http://www.nist.gov/customcf/get_pdf.cfm?pub_id=910136
Biometrics Identity Management JCD	Biometrics Support to Identity Management JCD, 31 Jan 2008.
Biometrics Identity Management JCD Body	Body of Biometrics in Support of Identity Management, Joint Capabilities Document (JCD), 31 Jan 2008.
Biometrics Identity Management JCD Glossary	Biometrics in Support of Identity Management, Joint Capabilities Document (JCD) Glossary, 4 Apr 2008.
CBEFF ANSI INCITS 398-2008	Common Biometric Exchange Formats Framework (CBEFF), ANSI INCITS 398-2008 http://webstore.ansi.org/RecordDetail.aspx?sku=ANSI+INCITS+398-2008
CJIS EBTS v9.4	Criminal Justice Information Services (CJIS) Electronic Fingerprint Transmission Specification (EBTS) Version 9.4, 12 Dec 2012. https://www.fbibiospecs.org/docs/EBTS_v9.4_FINAL_20121212_CLEAN.pdf
CONOPS for DoD Biometrics Identity Superiority	Capstone Concept of Operations for DoD Biometrics in Support of Identity Superiority, Nov 2006.
DA G2	Office of the Deputy Chief of Staff for Intelligence (ODCSINT) Department of the Army
DBIS	Defense Biometric Identification System (DBIDS) User Manual, 24 May 2006.
DFBA	Defense Forensics and Biometrics Agency http://www.biometrics.dod.mil
DNA	State of the Art Biometrics Excellence Roadmap Technology Assessment: Volume 3 DNA, Mar 2009.
DoD BEWL	The DOD Biometrically-enabled Watchlist (BEWL), A Revised Federated Approach, Aug 2009.
DoD Biometrics CONOPS	DOD Capstone Concept of Operations for Employing Biometrics in Military Operations, 10 Jun

2012.

DoD Biometrics Enterprise Strategic Plan	Department of Defense (DoD) Biometrics Enterprise Strategic Plan, 2008-2015, Final Draft, 12 Jun 2008.
DoD EBTS v2.0	Department of Defense (DoD) Electronic Biometric Transmission Specification (EBTS) Version 2.0, DIN: DOD_BTF_TS_EBTS_ Mar09_02.00.00, 27 March 2009.
DoDD 5400	DoD Directive 5400.11 and DoD 5400.11-R, 8 May 2007. http://www.dtic.mil/whs/directives/corres/pdf/540011p.pdf
DoDD 8521.01E	DoD Directive 8521.01E Enclosure 2 http://www.fas.org/irp/doddir/dod/d8521_01.pdf
DRS	Detainee Reporting System courtesy of National Detainee Reporting Center, Aug 2006.
EFS	Data Format for the Interchange of Extended Friction Ridge Features, 10 May 2010.
FBI NDIS	Federal Bureau of Investigation (FBI) website, National DNA Index System http://www.fbi.gov/about-us/lab/codis
FBI QA	Federal Bureau of Investigation (FBI) website, Quality Assurance Standards for DNA Databasing Laboratories http://www.fbi.gov/about-us/lab/codis/codis-and-ndis-fact-sheet
Fingerprint Sensor Product Guidelines	The Intel Corporation website, Biometric User Authentication: Fingerprint Sensor Product Guidelines
Handbook No. 11-25	Handbook No. 11-25. Commanders Guide to Biometrics in Afghanistan, Apr 2011.
iAfB	International Association for Biometrics (iAfB)
IBIA Glossary	International Biometrics & Identification Association Glossary (website) http://www.ibia.org/biometrics/glossary/
IDENT	Privacy Impact Assessment for the Automated Biometric Identification System (IDENT), 31 Jul 2006.
ISO/IEC 2382-37:2012(E)	ISO/IEC 2382-37:2012(E) First Edition, Information technology — Vocabulary — Part 37: Biometrics, 12 Dec 2012 http://standards.iso.org/ittf/PubliclyAvailableStandards/c055194_ISOIEC_2382-37_2012.zip
ISO/IEC SC37-n-3068	ISO/IEC JTC 1/SC 37 N 3068 SD2.11, Harmonized Biometric Vocabulary, 28 Feb 2009. http://isotc.iso.org/livelink/livelink/fetch/2000/2122/327993/2262372/2263033/2299739/JTC001-SC37-N-3068_SD_2_Version_11_January_2009.pdf?nodeid=7950678&vernum=0
JointPub	Joint Publication 1-02 Department of Defense Dictionary of Military and Associated Terms, 8 Nov 2010 (As Amended Through 15 Apr 2012). http://www.dtic.mil/doctrine/dod_dictionary

JPI CDD	Capability Development Document (CDD) for Joint Personal Identification (JPI)
Latent Fingerprint Matching	Latent Fingerprint Matching: Fusion of Rolled and Plain Fingerprints, ICB, Jun 2009. http://biometrics.cse.msu.edu/Publications/Fingerprint/FengYoonJain_FuseRollPlain_ICB09.pdf
New ABIS Improves Capability to Identify Terrorists Press Release	New Automated Biometric Identification System Improves Capability to Identify Terrorists Clarksburg, WV (press release BTF w/ PM Biometrics), 17 Feb 2009.
NIAP	National Information Assurance Partnership, US Government Biometric Verification Mode Protection Profile for Medium Robustness Environments v1.0, 15 Nov 2003.
NIST	National Institute of Standards and Technology (NIST) http://www.nist.gov/public_affairs/general_information.cfm
NIST/MINEX	National Institute of Standards and Technology / MINEX Webpage http://www.nist.gov/itl/iad/ig/minex.cfm
ODNI	Office of the Director of National Intelligence (ODNI)
PDES	U.S. Government Person Data Exchange Standard (PDES)
Report of the Defense Science Board Task Force on Defense Biometrics	Report of the Defense Science Board Task Force on Defense Biometrics, Mar 2007. http://www.acq.osd.mil/dsb/reports/ADA465930.pdf
SMT: Soft Biometric for Suspect and Victim Identification	Scars, Marks and Tattoos (SMT): Soft Biometric for Suspect and Victim Identification; Jung-Eun Lee, Anil K. Jain and Rong Jin; Biometrics Symposium 2008 http://www.cse.msu.edu/biometrics/Publications/SoftBiometrics/LeeJainJin_SMT_BSYM2008.pdf
SWGFAST Document #19, 24 Nov 2012	Scientific Working Group on Friction Ridge Analysis, Study and Technology (SWGFAST) Document #19 - Standard Terminology of Friction Ridge Examination v4.0, 24 Nov 2012 http://www.swgfast.org/Documents.html
TC 2-22.82 Biometrics-Enabled Intelligence	TC 2-22.82 Biometrics-Enabled Intelligence, Mar 2011.
TCD and BEC	BIOMETRICS TACTICAL COLLECTION DEVICE (TCD) AND BIOMETRICS ENTERPRISE CAPABILITY (BEC) ANALYSES OF ALTERNATIVES (AoAs), April 2010.
TWPDES	Intelligence Community Terrorist Watchlist Person Data Exchange Standard Data Element Dictionary, IC Metadata Working Group (IC MWG) Version 2.0, UNCLASSIFIED, 4 Jul 2005. https://www.niem.gov/documentsdb/Documents/Technical/TWPDES_3_final.zip
USACIL	U.S. Army Criminal Investigation Laboratory website http://www.cid.army.mil/usacil.html
USCENTCOM BISA	USCENTCOM Biometric Identification System for Access (BISA) CONOPS

CBV Core Term to DIV-2 Entity Mappings

Biometric Encounter	COLLECTION-ENCOUNTER
Biometric Identity	BIOMETRIC-SAMPLE-PERSON-IDENTITY
Biometric Sample	BIOMETRIC-SAMPLE
Biometrically Enabled Watchlist (BEWL)	PERSON-OF-INTEREST-LIST PERSON-OF-INTEREST-LIST-ENTRY PERSON BIOMETRIC-SAMPLE-PERSON-IDENTITY BIOMETRIC-SAMPLE
Identity	BIOMETRIC-REPOSITORY-IDENTITY
Latent Fingerprint	LATENT-PRINT-IMAGE
Latent Sample	LATENT-PRINT-IMAGE